NATURE'S MYSTERIES

LIGHTNING AND THUNDER

PAULA JOHANSON

Britannica® Educational Publishing
IN ASSOCIATION WITH
ROSEN EDUCATIONAL SERVICES

For my mother, who has been hit by lightning—twice

Published in 2019 by Britannica Educational Publishing (a trademark of Encyclopædia Britannica, Inc.) in association with
The Rosen Publishing Group, Inc.
29 East 21st Street, New York, NY 10010

Distributed exclusively by Rosen Publishing.
To see additional Britannica Educational Publishing titles, go to rosenpublishing.com.

First Edition

Britannica Educational Publishing
J.E. Luebering: Executive Director, Core Editorial
Mary Rose McCudden: Editor, Britannica Student Encyclopedia

Rosen Publishing
Kathy Kuhtz Campbell: Senior Editor
Michael Moy: Series Designer
Tahara Anderson: Book Layout
Cindy Reiman: Photography Manager
Sherri Jackson: Photo Researcher

Library of Congress Cataloging-in-Publication Data

Names: Johanson, Paula, author.
Title: Lightning and thunder / Paula Johanson.
Description: First edition. | New York: Britannica Educational Publishing, in Association with Rosen Educational Publishing, 2019 | Series: Nature's mysteries | Audience: Grades 1–5. | Includes glossary and index.
Identifiers: LCCN 2018014220| ISBN 9781508106630 (library bound) | ISBN 9781508106517 (pbk.) | ISBN 9781508106579 (6 pack)
Subjects: LCSH: Lightning—Juvenile literature. | Thunder—Juvenile literature. | Thunderstorms—Juvenile literature.
Classification: LCC QC966.5 .J64 2018 | DDC 551.56/32—dc21
LC record available at https://lccn.loc.gov/2018014220

Manufactured in the United States of America

Photo credits: Cover, p. 1 DeepDesertPhoto/RooM/Getty Images; p. 4 Steve Hardiman/iStock/Thinkstock; p. 5 Jhaz Phtography/Shutterstock.com; p. 6 QAI Publishing/Universal Images Group/Getty Images; p. 7 Stormchase/iStock/Thinkstock; p. 8 Designua/Shutterstock.com; pp. 9, 11 © Encyclopedia Britannica, Inc.; p. 10 Smebeesley/Shutterstock.com; p. 12 Everett Historical/Shutterstock.com; p. 13 Erik S. Lesser/Getty Images; p. 14 Abstract Aerial Art/Taxi/Getty Images; p. 15 Steve Cymro/Shutterstock.com; p. 16 Dziurek/Shutterstock.com; p. 17 Polonez/Shutterstock.com; p. 18 Jeff Greenberg/Universal Images Group/Getty Images; p. 19 Science Source/Getty Images; p. 20 Dariush M/Shutterstock.com; p. 21 Lukiyanova Natalia Frenta/Shutterstock.com; p. 22 Victor Habbick Visions/Science Photo Library/Getty Images; p. 23 Daniel L. Osborne/ Detlev van Ravenswaay/Science Source; p. 24 Encyclopedia Britannica/Universal Images Group/Getty Images; p. 25 Kenny Tong/Shutterstock.com; p. 26 AndyRogers23/Shutterstock.com; p. 27 Steven Puetzer/Photographer's Choice/Getty Images; p. 28 Science History Images/Alamy Stock Photo; p. 29 Julian Baum/Science Photo Library/Getty Images; interior pages background Mihai Simonia/Shutterstock.com.

CONTENTS

STORMY SKIES

Thunderstorms are a common weather disturbance. They are usually violent and short-lived. They almost always include thick clouds, heavy rain or hail, and strong winds. They also include lightning and thunder.

Thunderstorms occur in almost every region of the world. They usually include thick clouds, rain or hail, lightning, thunder, and strong winds.

In ancient times people believed that angry gods threw lightning bolts from the heavens. It was not until the 1700s that scientists offered an explanation for lightning. Lightning is **electricity** released from Earth's atmosphere during thunderstorms.

VOCABULARY

Electricity is the flow of tiny particles called electrons and protons. It can also mean the energy you get when electrons flow from place to place.

Lightning is most common in tropical regions. However, thunderstorms with lightning happen in almost every region of the world. An estimated 1,800 thunderstorms occur around the world at any given time. These storms produce eight million flashes of lightning each day.

If the electricity in one lightning bolt could be harnessed, it could power nearly sixty homes for one day.

Thunderstorms happen when hot, moist air rises quickly to cooler parts of the atmosphere. There, the air cools, and clouds and rain form. Lightning develops inside the clouds. As the lightning heats the air in its path, the air expands very quickly. The air then shrinks after the lightning is passed. This sudden air movement causes the sound of thunder. Meanwhile, cooled air sinks toward the ground. This movement of air causes heavy winds.

The stages of a thunderstorm include rising hot, moist air; the formation of clouds and rain; and the occurrence of lightning and thunder. When the air cools, the clouds sink and later disappear.

THINK ABOUT IT

Sunlight heating air causes winds and moisture to move, which can cause storms. On a small scale, water can be heated to boiling in a pot. What can you learn by looking at water boiling in a pot that can help you understand thunderstorms?

Some thunderstorms are severe enough to produce tornadoes. A tornado is a column of strongly rotating winds. It can produce winds as fast as 300 miles (483 kilometers) per hour.

Winds swirling around a moving storm can turn fast enough to form a tornado.

WHAT IS LIGHTNING?

Drops of water and ice inside clouds carry electrical charges. Some of these charges are positive and others are negative. Lightning occurs usually when too many negative charges build up in a cloud. Positive charges form under the cloud on the ground. These opposite charges are attracted to each other.

HOW LIGHTNING IS FORMED

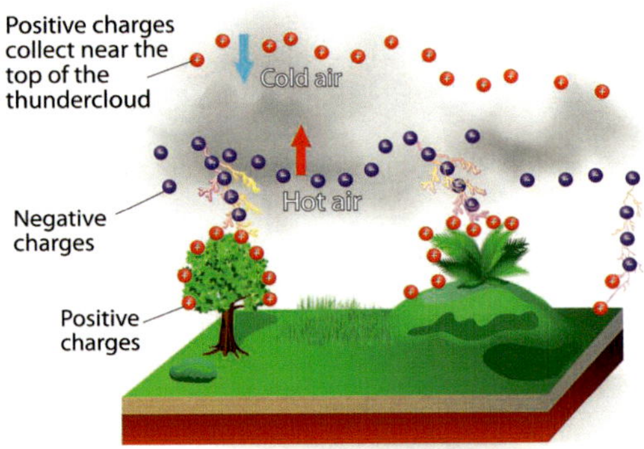

Charged particles will always flow in the direction where there are fewer particles of the same charge. The result can be a lightning bolt.

Electricity does not move easily through air. As the cloud grows, however, so does the strength of the charges. Eventually the cloud releases a strong, negatively charged

COMPARE AND CONTRAST

Movements of huge clouds can make lightning bolts. Moving your feet on a carpet can make a tiny spark when you touch a doorknob. How are these sparks alike? How are these electric sparks different?

electrical current. As the negative current heads toward the ground, a positively charged current jumps from the ground to meet it. When the currents join, a bright flash is created that heads back up toward the cloud.

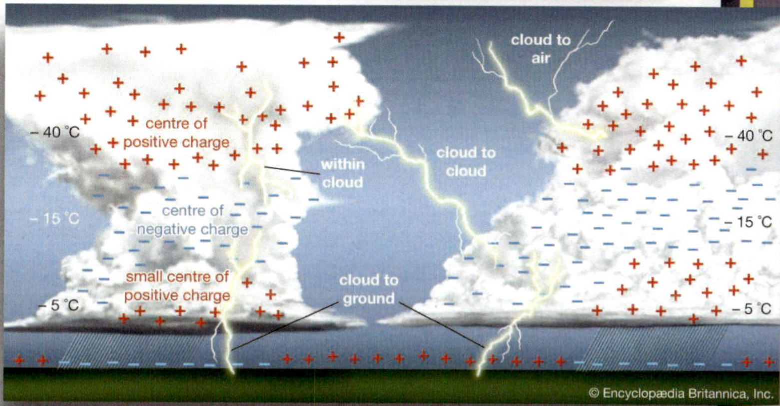

Lightning can travel from a cloud to the ground, within a cloud, between clouds, and from a cloud into the air.

That familiar sight is called cloud-to-ground lightning. Lightning can also occur within a cloud, between clouds, or between a cloud and the air. Each type of lightning is caused by the buildup and release of electrical charges.

WHAT IS THUNDER?

Lightning bolts flash first and are followed by rumbles of thunder from suddenly heated air.

The loud boom that follows a lightning flash is called thunder. People are often afraid of thunder, but it is just noise. Lightning is the dangerous part.

The electricity from the lightning heats the gases in the air. For a brief moment, a lightning bolt is hotter than the surface of the sun—about 54,000 degrees Fahrenheit (30,000 degrees Celsius). The

VOCABULARY

A shock wave is a pressure wave caused by a sudden movement.

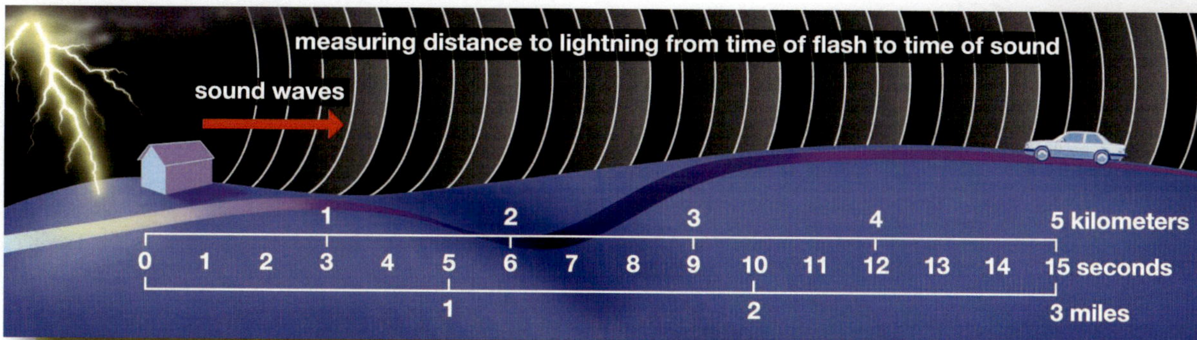

The time between seeing a flash of lightning and hearing thunder is about three seconds for each kilometer and five seconds for each mile.

air glows with heat! As the hot gases expand quickly, they make a loud noise. The hot air cools down just as quickly and makes a noise as it contracts. The **shock wave** of noise moves through the air. Thunder can be heard more than 10 miles (16 km) away from a lightning strike.

THE SCIENCE OF LIGHTNING

The ancient Greeks were the first to study electric forces. Much later, in the American colonies, Benjamin Franklin realized that lightning must be a discharge of electricity from clouds. To test his idea, Franklin flew a kite high in the air during a thunderstorm. A charge of electricity moved down the kite's wet string. Franklin proved his theory that lightning is electricity. However, that was a very dangerous experiment. Lightning is powerful, and people should avoid being near it.

In 1752, Benjamin Franklin used only a kite, a long string, and a key to prove his theory that lightning is electricity.

THINK ABOUT IT

People have been thinking about lightning for a very long time. What was different about the way Benjamin Franklin looked at that thunderstorm?

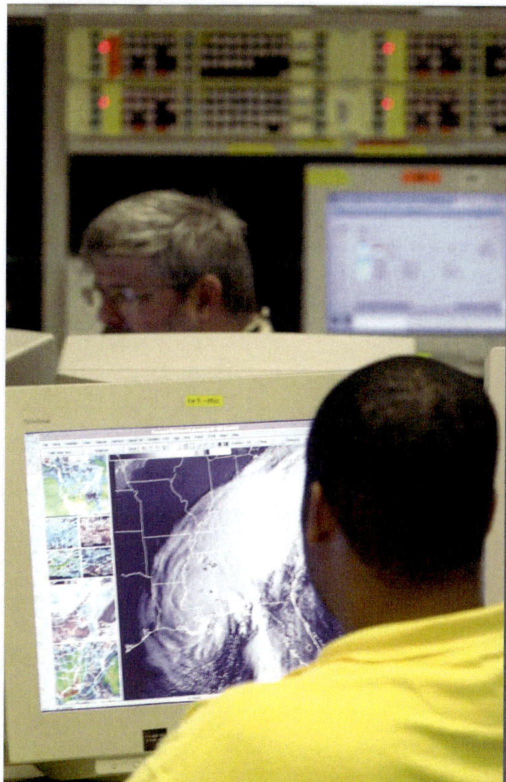

The study of lightning is still going on. Meteorologists are people who study weather and its causes. Meteorologists know they will have an opportunity to study lightning when they see huge, piled-up clouds called cumulonimbus clouds. Cumulonimbus clouds are the kinds of clouds that produce thunderstorms.

Meteorologists study and track movements of clouds and thunderstorms to help people prepare for danger.

EFFECTS OF LIGHTNING

Lightning can damage buildings, ships, and airplanes when it strikes. It can also kill or seriously injure a person. Lightning may strike wires or metal pipes and work its way into telephones or appliances. Lightning can also start forest fires or melt sand into a glassy mineral called fulgurite.

Wildfires around the world can be started by lightning that strikes dry trees, leaves, branches, or grass.

Lightning can also be useful. The heat from

COMPARE AND CONTRAST

Lightning is only one kind of danger in nature. Name some other kinds of danger in nature. Are they more or less dangerous than lightning? Do they have any useful effects like lightning?

lightning joins the nitrogen and oxygen in the air to form nitrates and other compounds. These nutrients fall to the ground when it rains. Earth's soil needs these nutrients to grow plants.

Lightning is part of a natural process called the nitrogen cycle. Nitrogen is important for the survival of life on Earth.

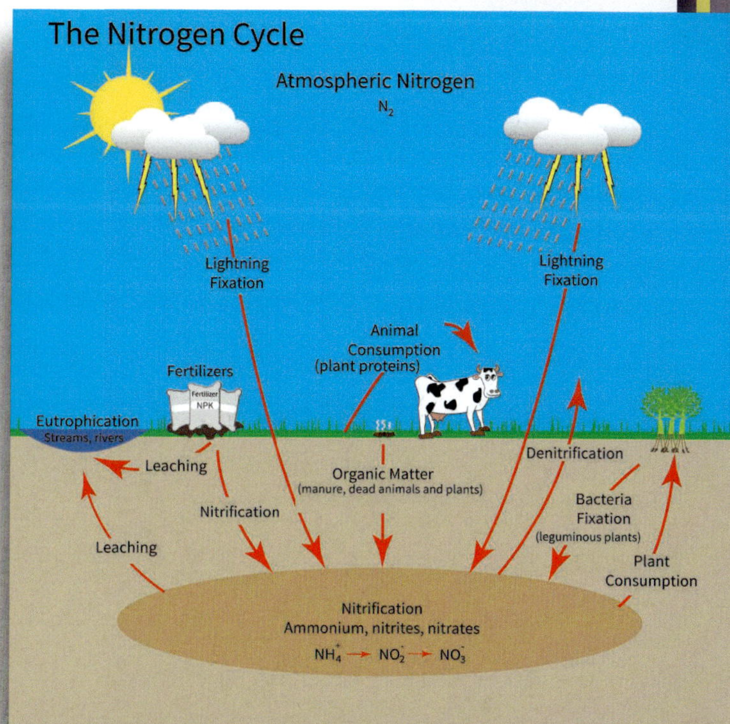

THE SPEED OF LIGHTNING AND THUNDER

A lightning bolt strikes in less than a second. The light from the flash, like all light, travels at a speed of about 186,000 miles (about 300,000 km) per second.

The speed of thunder is the speed that sound travels through air. That is about 1,129 feet (344 meters) per second, which is much

Here, sunlight is seen streaming through some clouds. The speed of light is much faster than the speed of sound.

THINK ABOUT IT

Why do you think you don't usually hear thunder at the same time you see a lightning flash? Think about how fast each one travels.

Lightning flashes are seen almost at once, but thunder takes more time to travel through air.

slower than the speed of light. It takes sound about five seconds to travel 1 mile (1,609 m). People who see a flash of lightning and want to know how far away it struck can count the seconds until they hear thunder. If there are ten seconds between the lightning and thunder, that means the lightning is 2 miles (3.2 km) away. The National Weather Service says if thunder can be heard, then lightning is close enough to strike. That is when it is time to find shelter.

THUNDERSTORM SAFETY

Lightning can hurt or kill a person. It is important to follow simple safety instructions during a thunderstorm. The sound of thunder is a warning that a storm is close enough to be dangerous.

If people are caught outside during a thunderstorm, they need to stay away from water and should not stand under a tall tree. Lightning tends to hit the highest object around. People are safer inside a building or a car and away

People need to be careful about lightning safety. Some places are more risky than others. A sign warns that a pier is dangerous during a storm.

THINK ABOUT IT

Being prepared for a thunderstorm helps people be safe. How can people be safe inside a building during a storm? What can they do to be safe if they are camping or playing sports outdoors?

from open doors, windows, and electrical appliances.

Benjamin Franklin's experiments with electricity led to his invention of lightning rods. These metal rods on roofs help protect buildings from lightning damage. The rod draws the lightning to it, and the lightning runs down a wire into the ground.

Benjamin Franklin put metal rods and wire on a home in Philadelphia to test his ideas on how to protect buildings from lightning damage.

WHEN EARTH WAS NEW

Millions of years ago there were no living things on Earth. Earth was very active though. There were many volcanoes as well as storms featuring thunder and lightning. Lightning flashes may have helped form the first living things.

In 1953 scientists made models of what they believed were the conditions on Earth before life existed. The scientists

When volcanoes erupt, rising clouds of steam, ash, and hot gases can sometimes cause lightning bolts.

VOCABULARY

Organic molecules are the building blocks of living things.

mixed water with gases thought to be in Earth's air at the time. The sealed containers were sparked with electricity, to act like lightning bolts. After several days, organic molecules were seen in the water. In many other experiments like this, the gases and water combined into **organic molecules**. The molecules that formed were some of the essential building blocks of life.

A photograph shows an amoeba, which is among the simplest of all living things. Billions of years ago, lightning made opportunities for life to begin.

HIGH-ALTITUDE LIGHTNING

High above thunderstorms, there are rare kinds of lightning. These kinds of lightning spark high into the air and last for much less than a second. They are rarely seen from the ground. They were not photographed before 1989. Scientists have given the forms names such as blue jets, red sprites, and elves.

High-altitude lightning does not look like ordinary bolts. Blue

Blue jets are lightning bolts that shoot out of the tops of thunderstorm clouds.

THINK ABOUT IT

Thunder and lightning always get people's attention. If people have always noticed lightning, why do you think it has been difficult to see and study high-altitude lightning until recently?

jets shoot above thunderstorms at about 60 miles (100 km) per second. Red sprites hang from 25 to 50 miles (40 to 80 km) above some thunderstorms. Elves form big rings hovering about 60 miles (100 km) above thunderstorms, spreading to 186 miles (300 km) across. Other strange forms of lightning are called trolls, pixies, and gnomes.

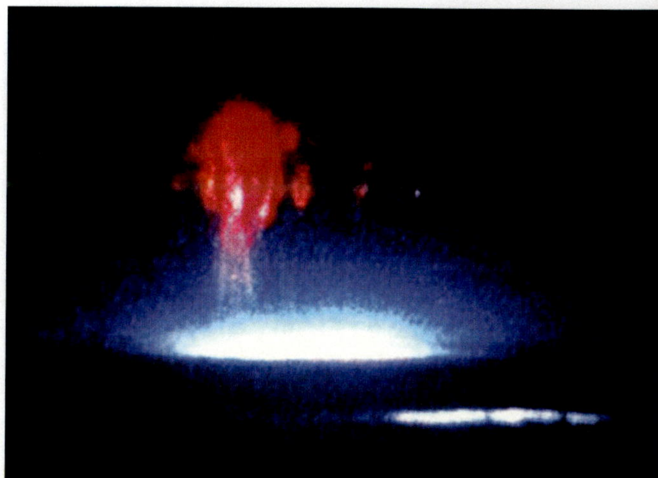

Red sprites last for only fractions of a second. They are thought to be caused by a rare form of lightning called positive lightning.

TRADITIONAL BELIEFS

In ancient Greek **mythology**, the most powerful god was Zeus. Romans later called him Jupiter. Zeus hurled lightning called thunderbolts at his enemies and at humans who angered him. These thunderbolts were made for him by a god called Hephaestus, or Vulcan in Roman mythology.

In Norse, or Viking, mythology, the god of thunder was Thor. In battles, Thor struck with a mighty hammer that gave off lightning bolts. The wheels of Thor's chariot rumbled to make the sound of thunder and sent out sparks as lightning.

The ancient Greeks believed Zeus ruled over humans and all the gods. He sent thunder, lightning, rain, and winds down to Earth.

VOCABULARY

Mythology is a collection of myths, or stories that tell how the world was created and why certain things happen. Many myths describe the actions of superhuman beings.

The Norse people believed that when the ground was struck by lightning, Thor had sent his hammer crashing to the earth. Traditional beliefs among many native North Americans still speak of thunderbirds, powerful spirits that change into birds huge enough to hunt whales. Lightning flashes out from thunderbirds' eyes, beaks, or wings, and the beat of their wings causes the rumble of thunder.

Thunderbirds are a popular symbol in Native American art. This totem pole stands in Stanley Park in Vancouver, British Columbia.

FACT OR FICTION?

There is an old saying that "lightning never strikes twice in the same place." That saying is not true! Lightning rods can be struck more than once.

Other people might say that a sudden event "struck like a bolt from the blue." That comes from the fact that lightning can strike up to 10 miles (16 km) away from a storm, from a sky that seems clear.

Sheet lightning is lightning that is enclosed within a cloud. It can make entire storm clouds glow in the night sky.

Some people believe "heat lightning" and "sheet lightning" are not dangerous. These are forms of lightning that are too far away to hear

VOCABULARY

Lightning bugs are also called fireflies. They use their light to make a certain series of flashes to attract a mate. When a possible mate sees the flashes, it returns the signal.

the thunder or that are only seen within clouds. They may not be dangerous at the time they are seen, but storms move or change rapidly, so be prepared to seek shelter.

Insects called **lightning bugs** can also be confusing. In spite of their name, lightning bugs have nothing to do with lightning. They are night-flying beetles that produce a bright soft flashing light for courtship purposes.

Lightning bugs have special organs that make light. These organs mix chemicals with oxygen from the air and release flashes of light.

UNDERSTANDING THUNDER AND LIGHTNING

Saint Elmo's fire is shown here on the masts of a ship at sea. This type of light is often seen before and after storms.

For many years people have told stories to try to explain the mysteries of lightning and thunder. In some Native American traditions, people who survived being struck by lightning often became shamans. They were believed to have received the power of the thunderbird. The thunderbird was a creature that was thought to create lightning and thunder.

People who worked outdoors worried about dangerous thunderstorms. Saint Elmo's fire is a light appearing on ship masts before and after thunderstorms.

THINK ABOUT IT

The story of "Rip Van Winkle" told that thunder was made by little people in the hills who threw balls and knocked down bowling pins. How does this story and others like it try to make sense of mysterious thunder?

Sailors believed this electric glow was a sign that their patron saint was protecting them.

Ball lightning is so rare that it is hard for scientists to learn how to study it.

Ball lightning is something no one understands. It can burn or melt things but is usually harmless. These small glowing balls occur near the ground during thunderstorms. Scientists do not just make up stories about lightning. They observe storms and propose theories to explain what they can understand.

GLOSSARY

CONTRACT To make or become smaller.

CURRENT A stream of electric charge.

ELECTRON A tiny particle that has a negative charge of electricity and travels around the nucleus of an atom. Atoms are the building blocks of all things.

EXPERIMENT A procedure or action carried out under controlled conditions in order to discover something or test an idea.

INVENTION A new kind of thing or process a person has made.

LIGHTNING ROD A metal rod set up on a building or a ship and connected with the earth or water below to decrease the chances of damage from lightning.

METEOROLOGY The science that deals with the atmosphere, weather, and weather forecasting.

PROTON A tiny particle that has a positive charge of electricity and travels around the nucleus of an atom. Atoms are the building blocks of all things.

SHAMAN A healer who is believed to have special powers.

THEORIES Explanations for why things work or how things happen. Theories are based on ideas that can be tested.

THUNDERBOLT A flash of lightning and the thunder that follows it.

TRADITIONAL Handed down from one generation to another.

TROPICAL REGIONS Areas of Earth that are warm or hot throughout the year.

VOLCANO A vent or crack in Earth's crust from which melted or hot rock and steam come out.

WEATHER The daily state of the air and atmosphere at a particular time and place. It can be calm or windy, bright sunshine, or storming with rain, hail, or snow.

FOR MORE INFORMATION

Books

Gerry, Lisa M. *Weather* (Explore My World). Washington, DC: National Geographic Kids, 2018.

Greek, Joe. *Weather and Climate* (Let's Find Out! Our Dynamic Earth). New York, NY: Britannica Educational Publishing, 2018.

Johnson, Robin. *What Is a Thunderstorm?* (Severe Weather Close-Up). New York, NY: Crabtree Publishing Company, 2016.

Randolph, Joanne. *What Are the Elements of the Weather?* (Let's Find Out! Weather and Climate). New York, NY: Britannica Educational Publishing, 2015.

Rivera, Andrea. *Thunder & Lightning.* Minneapolis, MN: ABDO Zoom, 2017.

Salzmann, Mary Elizabeth. *Benjamin Franklin* (Scientists at Work). Minneapolis, MN: ABDO Publishing, 2017.

VanVoorst, Jenny Fretland. *Lightning*. Minneapolis, MN: Bullfrog Books, 2017.

Websites

Easy Science for Kids

"Thunder and Lightning"

http://easyscienceforkids.com/all-about-thunder-and-lightning/

National Geographic Kids

"Lightning"

https://kids.nationalgeographic.com/explore/science/lightning/#lightning-trees.jpg

PBS LearningMedia

"Lightning!"

https://ny.pbslearningmedia.org/resource/phy03.sci.phys.mfw.lightning/lightning/#.WqvfcGaZO-o

INDEX